KRAPP'S LAST TAPE and EMBERS

by the same author

*

by Samuel Beckett
and others

KRAPP'S LAST TAPE
and
EMBERS

*

SAMUEL BECKETT

FABER AND FABER
London · Boston

First published in 1959
by Faber and Faber Limited
3 Queen Square London WC1
First published in this edition 1965
Reprinted in 1966, 1968, 1970, 1973,1976 and 1979
Printed in Great Britain by
Whitstable Litho Ltd Whitstable Kent
All rights reserved
© Samuel Beckett
Krapp's Last Tape 1958
Embers 1959

ISBN 0 571 06209 1

All applications for performing rights in *Krapp's Last Tape* and *Embers* should be addressed to Curtis Brown Ltd., 13 King Street, London, WC2.

The first performance in Great Britain of *Krapp's Last Tape* was given at the Royal Court Theatre, Sloane Square, London, on 28th October 1958. It was directed by Donald McWhinnie; and Krapp was played by Patrick Magee.

Embers, a new play specially written for broadcasting, was first performed in the Third Programme on 24th June 1959. The cast was as follows:

Henry	Jack MacGowran
Ada	Kathleen Michael
Addie	Kathleen Helme
The Music Master and The Riding Master	Patrick Magee

Pianist: Cicely Hoye

Produced by Donald McWhinnie

KRAPP'S LAST TAPE

*

A late evening in the future.

KRAPP's *den.*

Front centre a small table, the two drawers of which open towards the audience.

Sitting at the table, facing front, i.e. across from the drawers, a wearish old man: KRAPP.

Rusty black narrow trousers too short for him. Rusty black sleeveless waistcoat, four capacious pockets. Heavy silver watch and chain. Grimy white shirt open at neck, no collar. Surprising pair of dirty white boots, size ten at least, very narrow and pointed.

White face. Purple nose. Disordered grey hair. Unshaven.

Very near-sighted (but unspectacled). Hard of hearing.

Cracked voice. Distinctive intonation.

Laborious walk.

On the table a tape-recorder with microphone and a number of cardboard boxes containing reels of recorded tapes.

Table and immediately adjacent area in strong white light. Rest of stage in darkness.

KRAPP *remains a moment motionless, heaves a great sigh, looks at his watch, fumbles in his pockets, takes out an envelope, puts it back, fumbles, takes out a small bunch of keys, raises it to his eyes, chooses a key, gets up and moves to front of table. He stoops, unlocks first drawer, peers into it, feels about inside it, takes out a reel of tape, peers at it, puts it back, locks drawer, unlocks second drawer, peers into it, feels about inside it, takes out a large banana, peers at*

9

it, locks drawer, puts keys back in his pocket. He turns, advances to edge of stage, halts, strokes banana, peels it, drops skin at his feet, puts end of banana in his mouth and remains motionless, staring vacuously before him. Finally he bites off the end, turns aside and begins pacing to and fro at edge of stage, in the light, i.e. not more than four or five paces either way, meditatively eating banana. He treads on skin, slips, nearly falls, recovers himself, stoops and peers at skin and finally pushes it, still stooping, with his foot over edge of stage into pit. He resumes his pacing, finishes banana, returns to table, sits down, remains a moment motionless, heaves a great sigh, takes keys from his pockets, raises them to his eyes, chooses key, gets up and moves to front of table, unlocks second drawer, takes out a second large banana, peers at it, locks drawer, puts back keys in his pocket, turns, advances to edge of stage, halts, strokes banana, peels it, tosses skin into pit, puts end of banana in his mouth and remains motionless, staring vacuously before him. Finally he has an idea, puts banana in his waistcoat pocket, the end emerging, and goes with all the speed he can muster backstage into darkness. Ten seconds. Loud pop of cork. Fifteen seconds. He comes back into light carrying an old ledger and sits down at table. He lays ledger on table, wipes his mouth, wipes his hands on the front of his waistcoat, brings them smartly together and rubs them.

KRAPP: *(briskly).* Ah! *(He bends over ledger, turns the pages, finds the entry he wants, reads.)* Box . . . thrree . . . spool . . . five. *(He raises his head and stares front. With relish.)* Spool! *(Pause.)* Spooool! *(Happy smile. Pause. He bends over table, starts peering and poking at the boxes.)* Box . . . thrree . . . thrree . . . four . . . two . . . *(with surprise)* nine! good God! . . . seven . . . ah! the little rascal! *(He takes up box, peers at it.)* Box thrree. *(He lays it on table, opens it and peers at spools inside.)* Spool . . . *(he peers at ledger)* . . . five . . . *(he peers at*

spools) . . . five . . . five . . . ah! the little scoundrel! (*He takes out a spool, peers at it.*) Spool five. (*He lays it on table, closes box three, puts it back with the others, takes up the spool.*) Box thrree, spool five. (*He bends over the machine, looks up. With relish.*) Spooool! (*Happy smile. He bends, loads spool on machine, rubs his hands.*) Ah! (*He peers at ledger, reads entry at foot of page.*) Mother at rest at last. . . . Hm. . . . The black ball. . . . (*He raises his head, stares blankly front. Puzzled.*) Black ball? . . . (*He peers again at ledger, reads.*) The dark nurse. . . . (*He raises his head, broods, peers again at ledger, reads.*) Slight improvement in bowel condition. . . . Hm. . . . Memorable . . . what? (*He peers closer.*) Equinox, memorable equinox. (*He raises his head, stares blankly front. Puzzled.*) Memorable equinox? . . . (*Pause. He shrugs his shoulders, peers again at ledger, reads.*) Farewell to—(*he turns page*)—love.
He raises his head, broods, bends over machine, switches on and assumes listening posture, i.e. leaning forward, elbows on table, hand cupping ear towards machine, face front.

TAPE: (*strong voice, rather pompous, clearly Krapp's at a much earlier time*). Thirty-nine today, sound as a—(*Settling himself more comfortably he knocks one of the boxes off the table, curses, switches off, sweeps boxes and ledger violently to the ground, winds tape back to beginning, switches on, resumes posture.*) Thirty-nine today, sound as a bell, apart from my old weakness, and intellectually I have now every reason to suspect at the . . . (*hesitates*) . . . crest of the wave—or thereabouts. Celebrated the awful occasion, as in recent years, quietly at the Winehouse. Not a soul. Sat before the fire with closed eyes, separating the grain from the husks. Jotted down a few notes, on the back of an envelope. Good to be back in my den, in my old rags. Have just eaten I regret to say three bananas and only with difficulty refrained from a fourth. Fatal things for a man with my condition. (*Vehemently.*) Cut 'em out! (*Pause.*) The new light above my table is a great improvement. With all this darkness round me I feel less alone. (*Pause.*) In a way. (*Pause.*) I love to get up and move about in it, then back here to . . . (*hesitates*) . . . me. (*Pause.*) Krapp.

Pause.

The grain, now what I wonder do I mean by that, I mean . . . (*hesitates*) . . . I suppose I mean those things worth having when all the dust has—when all *my* dust has settled. I close my eyes and try and imagine them.

Pause. KRAPP *closes his eyes briefly.*

Extraordinary silence this evening, I strain my ears and do not hear a sound. Old Miss McGlome always sings at this hour. But not tonight. Songs of her girlhood, she says. Hard to think of her as a girl. Wonderful woman though. Connaught, I fancy. (*Pause.*) Shall I sing when I am her age, if I ever am? No. (*Pause.*) Did I sing as a boy? No. (*Pause.*) Did I ever sing? No.

Pause.

Just been listening to an old year, passages at random. I did not check in the book, but it must be at least ten or twelve years ago. At that time I think I was still living on and off with Bianca in Kedar Street. Well out of that, Jesus yes! Hopeless business. (*Pause.*) Not much about her, apart from a tribute to her eyes. Very warm. I

suddenly saw them again. (*Pause.*) Incomparable! (*Pause.*)
Ah well. . . . (*Pause.*) These old P.M.s are gruesome, but
I often find them—(KRAPP *switches off, broods, switches
on*)—a help before embarking on a new . . . (hesitates)
. . . retrospect. Hard to believe I was ever that young
whelp. The voice! Jesus! And the aspirations! (*Brief
laugh in which* KRAPP *joins.*) And the resolutions! (*Brief
laugh in which* KRAPP *joins.*) To drink less, in particular.
(*Brief laugh of* KRAPP *alone.*) Statistics. Seventeen
hundred hours, out of the preceding eight thousand odd,
consumed on licensed premises alone. More than 20 per
cent, say 40 per cent of his waking life. (*Pause.*) Plans
for a less . . . (hesitates) . . . engrossing sexual life. Last
illness of his father. Flagging pursuit of happiness.
Unattainable laxation. Sneers at what he calls his youth
and thanks to God that it's over. (*Pause.*) False ring
there. (*Pause.*) Shadows of the opus . . . magnum.
Closing with a—(*brief laugh*)—yelp to Providence.
(*Prolonged laugh in which* KRAPP *joins.*) What remains of
all that misery? A girl in a shabby green coat, on a
railway-station platform? No?

Pause.

When I look—

KRAPP *switches off, broods, looks at his watch, gets up,
goes backstage into darkness. Ten seconds. Pop of cork.
Ten seconds. Second cork. Ten seconds. Third cork.
Ten seconds. Brief burst of quavering song.*

KRAPP: (*sings*).   Now the day is over,
                    Night is drawing nigh-igh,
                    Shadows—

KRAPP'S LAST TAPE

Fit of coughing. He comes back into light, sits down, wipes his mouth, switches on, resumes his listening posture.

TAPE: —back on the year that is gone, with what I hope is perhaps a glint of the old eye to come, there is of course the house on the canal where mother lay a-dying, in the late autumn, after her long viduity (KRAPP *gives a start*), and the—(KRAPP *switches off, winds back tape a little, bends his ear closer to machine, switches on*)— a-dying, after her long viduity, and the—

KRAPP *switches off, raises his head, stares blankly before him. His lips move in the syllables of 'viduity'. No sound. He gets up, goes backstage into darkness, comes back with an enormous dictionary, lays it on table, sits down and looks up the word.*

KRAPP: (*reading from dictionary*). State—or condition—of being —or remaining—a widow—or widower. (*Looks up. Puzzled.*) Being—or remaining? . . . (*Pause. He peers again at dictionary. Reading.*) 'Deep weeds of viduity.' . . . Also of an animal, especially a bird . . . the vidua or weaver-bird. . . . Black plumage of male. . . . (*He looks up. With relish.*) The vidua-bird!

Pause. He closes dictionary, switches on, resumes listening posture.

TAPE: —bench by the weir from where I could see her window. There I sat, in the biting wind, wishing she were gone. (*Pause.*) Hardly a soul, just a few regulars, nursemaids, infants, old men, dogs, I got to know them quite well— oh by appearance of course I mean! One dark young beauty I recollect particularly, all white and starch,

14

incomparable bosom, with a big black hooded
perambulator, most funereal thing. Whenever I looked
in her direction she had her eyes on me. And yet when
I was bold enough to speak to her—not having been
introduced—she threatened to call a policeman. As if I
had designs on her virtue! (*Laugh. Pause.*) The face she
had! The eyes! Like . . . (*hesitates*) . . . chrysolite!
(*Pause.*) Ah well. . . . (*Pause.*) I was there when—
(KRAPP *switches off, broods, switches on again*)—the
blind went down, one of those dirty brown roller affairs,
throwing a ball for a little white dog as chance would
have it. I happened to look up and there it was. All
over and done with, at last. I sat on for a few moments
with the ball in my hand and the dog yelping and
pawing at me. (*Pause.*) Moments. Her moments, my
moments. (*Pause.*) The dog's moments. (*Pause.*) In the
end I held it out to him and he took it in his mouth,
gently, gently. A small, old, black, hard, solid rubber
ball. (*Pause.*) I shall feel it, in my hand, until my dying
day. (*Pause.*) I might have kept it. (*Pause.*) But I gave it
to the dog.

Pause.

Ah well. . . .

Pause.

Spiritually a year of profound gloom and indigence until
that memorable night in March, at the end of the jetty,
in the howling wind, never to be forgotten, when
suddenly I saw the whole thing. The vision at last. This
I fancy is what I have chiefly to record this evening,
against the day when my work will be done and perhaps
no place left in my memory, warm or cold, for the

miracle that . . . (*hesitates*) . . . for the fire that set it alight. What I suddenly saw then was this, that the belief I had been going on all my life, namely—(KRAPP *switches off impatiently, winds tape forward, switches on again*)—great granite rocks the foam flying up in the light of the lighthouse and the wind-gauge spinning like a propeller, clear to me at last that the dark I have always struggled to keep under is in reality my most—(KRAPP *curses, switches off, winds tape forward, switches on again*)—unshatterable association until my dissolution of storm and night with the light of the understanding and the fire—(KRAPP *curses louder, switches off, winds tape forward, switches on again*—my face in her breasts and my hand on her. We lay there without moving. But under us all moved, and moved us, gently, up and down, and from side to side.

Pause.

Past midnight. Never knew such silence. The earth might be uninhabited.

Pause.

Here I end—

KRAPP *switches off, winds tape back, switches on again.*
—upper lake, with the punt, bathed off the bank, then pushed out into the stream and drifted. She lay stretched out on the floorboards with her hands under her head and her eyes closed. Sun blazing down, bit of a breeze, water nice and lively. I noticed a scratch on her thigh and asked her how she came by it. Picking gooseberries, she said. I said again I thought it was hopeless and no good going on and she agreed, without opening

her eyes. (*Pause.*) I asked her to look at me and after a few moments—(*pause*)—after a few moments she did, but the eyes just slits, because of the ġlare. I bent over her to get them in the shadow and they opened. (*Pause. Low.*) Let me in. (*Pause.*) We drifted in among the flags and stuck. The way they went down, sighing, before the stem! (*Pause.*) I lay down across her with my face in her breasts and my hand on her. We lay there without moving. But under us all moved, and moved us, gently, up and down, and from side to side.

Pause.

Past midnight. Never knew—

KRAPP *switches off, broods. Finally he fumbles in his pockets, encounters the banana, takes it out, peers at it, puts it back, fumbles, brings out envelope, fumbles, puts back envelope, looks at his watch, gets up and goes backstage into darkness. Ten seconds. Sound of bottle against glass, then brief siphon. Ten seconds. Bottle against glass alone. Ten seconds. He comes back a little unsteadily into light, goes to front of table, takes out keys, raises them to his eyes, chooses key, unlocks first drawer, peers into it, feels about inside, takes out reel, peers at it, locks drawer, puts keys back in his pocket, goes and sits down, takes reel off machine, lays it on dictionary, loads virgin reel on machine, takes envelope from his pocket, consults back of it, lays it on table, switches on, clears his throat and begins to record.*

KRAPP: Just been listening to that stupid bastard I took myself for thirty years ago, hard to believe I was ever as bad as that. Thank God that's all done with anyway. (*Pause.*)

The eyes she had! (*Broods, realizes he is recording silence, switches off, broods. Finally.*) Everything there, everything, all the—(*Realizes this is not being recorded, switches on.*) Everything there, everything on this old muckball, all the light and dark and famine and feasting of . . . (*hesitates*) . . . the ages! (*In a shout.*) Yes! (*Pause.*) Let that go! Jesus! Take his mind off his homework! Jesus! (*Pause. Weary.*) Ah well, maybe he was right. (*Pause.*) Maybe he was right. (*Broods. Realizes. Switches off. Consults envelope.*) Pah! (*Crumples it and throws it away. Broods. Switches on.*) Nothing to say, not a squeak. What's a year now? The sour cud and the iron stool. (*Pause.*) Revelled in the word spool. (*With relish.*) Spooool! Happiest moment of the past half million. (*Pause.*) Seventeen copies sold, of which eleven at trade price to free circulating libraries beyond the seas. Getting known. (*Pause.*) One pound six and something, eight I have little doubt. (*Pause.*) Crawled out once or twice, before the summer was cold. Sat shivering in the park, drowned in dreams and burning to be gone. Not a soul. (*Pause.*) Last fancies. (*Vehemently.*) Keep 'em under! (*Pause.*) Scalded the eyes out of me reading *Effie* again, a page a day, with tears again. Effie. . . . (*Pause.*) Could have been happy with her, up there on the Baltic, and the pines, and the dunes. (*Pause.*) Could I? (*Pause.*) And she? (*Pause.*) Pah! (*Pause.*) Fanny came in a couple of times. Bony old ghost of a whore. Couldn't do much, but I suppose better than a kick in the crutch. The last time wasn't so bad. How do you manage it, she said, at your age? I told her I'd been saving up for her all my life. (*Pause.*) Went to Vespers once, like when I was in short trousers. (*Pause. Sings.*)

Now the day is over,
Night is drawing nigh-igh,
Shadows—(*coughing, then almost inaudible*)—
    of the evening
Steal across the sky.

(*Gasping.*) Went to sleep and fell off the pew. (*Pause.*)
Sometimes wondered in the night if a last effort mightn't
—(*Pause.*) Ah finish your booze now and get to your
bed. Go on with this drivel in the morning. Or leave it
at that. (*Pause.*) Leave it at that. (*Pause.*) Lie propped
up in the dark—and wander. Be again in the dingle on a
Christmas Eve, gathering holly, the red-berried. (*Pause.*)
Be again on Croghan on a Sunday morning, in the haze,
with the bitch, stop and listen to the bells. (*Pause.*) And
so on. (*Pause.*) Be again, be again. (*Pause.*) All that old
misery. (*Pause.*) Once wasn't enough for you. (*Pause.*)
Lie down across her.

*Long pause. He suddenly bends over machine, switches
off, wrenches off tape, throws it away, puts on the other,
winds it forward to the passage he wants, switches on,
listens staring front.*

TAPE: —gooseberries, she said. I said again I thought it was
    hopeless and no good going on and she agreed,
    without opening her eyes. (*Pause.*) I asked her to look at
    me and after a few moments—(*pause*)—after a few
    moments she did, but the eyes just slits, because of the
    glare. I bent over her to get them in the shadow and
    they opened. (*Pause. Low.*) Let me in. (*Pause.*) We
    drifted in among the flags and stuck. The way they went
    down, sighing, before the stem! (*Pause.*) I lay down
    across her with my face in her breasts and my hand on

her. We lay there without moving. But under us all moved, and moved us, gently, up and down, and from side to side.

Pause. KRAPP's *lips move. No sound.*

Past midnight. Never knew such silence. The earth might be uninhabited.

Pause.

Here I end this reel. Box—(*pause*)—three, spool—(*pause*)—five. (*Pause.*) Perhaps my best years are gone. When there was a chance of happiness. But I wouldn't want them back. Not with the fire in me now. No, I wouldn't want them back.

KRAPP *motionless staring before him. The tape runs on in silence.*

CURTAIN

EMBERS

*

Sea scarcely audible.
Henry's boots on shingle. He halts.
Sea a little louder.

HENRY: On. (*Sea. Voice louder.*) On! (*He moves on. Boots on shingle. As he goes.*) Stop. (*Boots on shingle. As he goes, louder.*) Stop! (*He halts. Sea a little louder.*) Down. (*Sea. Voice louder.*) Down! (*Slither of shingle as he sits. Sea, still faint, audible throughout what follows whenever pause indicated.*) Who is beside me now? (*Pause.*) An old man, blind and foolish. (*Pause.*) My father, back from the dead, to be with me. (*Pause.*) As if he hadn't died. (*Pause.*) No, simply back from the dead, to be with me, in this strange place. (*Pause.*) Can he hear me? (*Pause.*) Yes, he must hear me. (*Pause.*) To answer me? (*Pause.*) No, he doesn't answer me. (*Pause.*) Just be with me. (*Pause.*) That sound you hear is the sea. (*Pause. Louder.*) I say that sound you hear is the sea, we are sitting on the strand. (*Pause.*) I mention it because the sound is so strange, so unlike the sound of the sea, that if you didn't see what it was you wouldn't know what it was. (*Pause.*) Hooves! (*Pause. Louder.*) Hooves! (*Sound of*
21

*hooves walking on hard road. They die rapidly
away. Pause.*) Again! (*Hooves as before. Pause.
Excitedly.*) Train it to mark time! Shoe it with
steel and tie it up in the yard, have it stamp all
day! (*Pause.*) A ten-ton mammoth back from
the dead, shoe it with steel and have it tramp
the world down! (*Pause.*) Listen to it! (*Pause.*)
Listen to the light now, you always loved light,
not long past noon and all the shore in shadow
and the sea out as far as the island. (*Pause.*) You
would never live this side of the bay, you wanted
the sun on the water for that evening bathe you
took once too often. But when I got your money
I moved across, as perhaps you may know.
(*Pause.*) We never found your body, you know,
that held up probate an unconscionable time,
they said there was nothing to prove you hadn't
run away from us all and alive and well under a
false name in the Argentine for example, that
grieved mother greatly. (*Pause.*) I'm like you in
that, can't stay away from it, but I never go in,
no, I think the last time I went in was with you.
(*Pause.*) Just be near it. (*Pause.*) Today it's calm,
but I often hear it above in the house and
walking the roads and start talking, oh just loud
enough to drown it, nobody notices. (*Pause.*)
But I'd be talking now no matter where I was,
I once went to Switzerland to get away from the
cursed thing and never stopped all the time I was
there. (*Pause.*) I usen't to need anyone, just to
myself, stories, there was a great one about an
old fellow called Bolton, I never finished it, I
never finished any of them, I never finished

anything, everything always went on for ever.
(*Pause.*) Bolton. (*Pause. Louder.*) Bolton! (*Pause.*)
There before the fire. (*Pause.*) Before the fire
with all the shutters . . . no, hangings, hangings,
all the hangings drawn and the light, no light,
only the light of the fire, sitting there in the . . .
no, standing, standing there on the hearthrug
in the dark before the fire with his arms on the
chimney-piece and his head on his arms, standing
there waiting in the dark before the fire in his old
red dressing-gown and no sound in the house of
any kind, only the sound of the fire. (*Pause.*)
Standing there in his old red dressing-gown
might go on fire any minute like when he was a
child, no, that was his pyjamas, standing there
waiting in the dark, no light, only the light of the
fire, and no sound of any kind, only the fire, an
old man in great trouble. (*Pause.*) Ring then at
the door and over he goes to the window and
looks out between the hangings, fine old chap,
very big and strong, bright winter's night, snow
everywhere, bitter cold, white world, cedar
boughs bending under load, and then as the arm
goes up to ring again recognizes . . . Holloway
. . . (*long pause*) . . . yes, Holloway, recognizes
Holloway, goes down and opens. (*Pause.*)
Outside all still, not a sound, dog's chain maybe
or a bough groaning if you stood there listening
long enough, white world, Holloway with his
little black bag, not a sound, bitter cold, full
moon small and white, crooked trail of
Holloway's galoshes, Vega in the Lyre very
green. (*Pause.*) Vega in the Lyre very green.

(*Pause.*) Following conversation then on the
step, no, in the room, back in the room, following
conversation then back in the room, Holloway:
'My dear Bolton, it is now past midnight, if you
would be good enough—', gets no further,
Bolton: 'Please! PLEASE!' Dead silence then,
not a sound, only the fire, all coal, burning
down now, Holloway on the hearthrug trying to
toast his arse, Bolton, where's Bolton, no light,
only the fire, Bolton at the window, his back to
the hangings, holding them a little apart with
his hand, looking out, white world, even the
spire, white to the vane, most unusual, silence in
the house, not a sound, only the fire, no flames
now, embers. (*Pause.*) Embers. (*Pause.*) Shifting,
lapsing, furtive like, dreadful sound, Holloway
on the rug, fine old chap, six foot, burly, legs
apart, hands behind his back holding up the
tails of his old macfarlane, Bolton at the
window, grand old figure in his old red
dressing-gown, back against the hangings, hand
stretched out widening the chink, looking out,
white world, great trouble, not a sound, only the
embers, sound of dying, dying glow, Holloway,
Bolton, Bolton, Holloway, old men, great
trouble, white world, not a sound. (*Pause.*)
Listen to it! (*Pause.*) Close your eyes and listen
to it, what would you think it was? (*Pause.
Vehement.*) A drip! A drip! (*Sound of drip,
rapidly amplified, suddenly cut off.*) Again! (*Drip
again. Amplification begins.*) No! (*Drip cut off.
Pause.*) Father! (*Pause. Agitated.*) Stories, stories,
years and years of stories, till the need came on

24

me, for someone, to be with me, anyone, a
stranger, to talk to, imagine he hears me, years
of that, and then, now, for someone who . . .
knew me, in the old days, anyone, to be with
me, imagine he hears me, what I am, now.
(*Pause.*) No good either. (*Pause.*) Not
there either. (*Pause.*) Try again. (*Pause.*)
White world, not a sound. (*Pause.*) Holloway.
(*Pause.*) Holloway says he'll go, damned if he'll
sit up all night before a black grate, doesn't
understand, call a man out, an old friend, in the
cold and dark, an old friend, urgent need, bring
the bag, then not a word, no explanation, no
heat, no light, Bolton: 'Please! PLEASE!'
Holloway, no refreshment, no welcome, chilled
to the medulla, catch his death, can't understand,
strange treatment, old friend, says he'll go,
doesn't move, not a sound, fire dying, white
beam from window, ghastly scene, wishes to
God he hadn't come, no good, fire out, bitter
cold, great trouble, white world, not a sound, no
good. (*Pause.*) No good. (*Pause.*) Can't do it.
(*Pause.*) Listen to it! (*Pause.*) Father! (*Pause.*)
You wouldn't know me now, you'd be sorry
you ever had me, but you were that already,
a washout, that's the last I heard from you, a
washout. (*Pause. Imitating father's voice.*) 'Are
you coming for a dip?' 'Come on, come
on.' 'No.' Glare, stump to door, turn, glare.
'A washout, that's all you are, a washout!'
(*Violent slam of door. Pause.*) Again! (*Slam.
Pause.*) Slam life shut like that! (*Pause.*)
Washout. (*Pause.*) Wish to Christ she had.

25

(*Pause.*) Never met Ada, did you, or did you, I can't remember, no matter, no one'd know her now. (*Pause.*) What turned her against me do you think, the child I suppose, horrid little creature, wish to God we'd never had her, I use to walk with her in the fields, Jesus that was awful, she wouldn't let go my hand and I mad to talk. 'Run along now, Addie, and look at the lambs.' (*Imitating* ADDIE'S *voice.*) 'No papa.' 'Go on now, go on.' (*Plaintive.*) 'No papa.' (*Violent.*) 'Go on with you when you're told and look at the lambs!' (ADDIE'S *loud wail. Pause.*) Ada too, conversation with her, that was something, that's what hell will be like, small chat to the babbling of Lethe about the good old days when we wished we were dead. (*Pause.*) Price of margarine fifty years ago. (*Pause.*) And now. (*Pause. With solemn indignation.*) Price of blueband now! (*Pause.*) Father! (*Pause.*) Tired of talking to you. (*Pause.*) That was always the way, walk all over the mountains with you talking and talking and then suddenly mum and home in misery and not a word to a soul for weeks, sulky little bastard, better off dead, better off dead. (*Long pause.*) Ada. (*Pause. Louder.*) Ada!

ADA: (*low remote voice throughout*). Yes.

HENRY: Have you been there long?

ADA: Some little time. (*Pause.*) Why do you stop, don't mind me. (*Pause.*) Do you want me to go away? (*Pause.*) Where is Addie?

Pause.

HENRY: With her music master. (*Pause.*) Are you going to answer me today?

ADA: You shouldn't be sitting on the cold stones, they're bad for your growths. Raise yourself up till I slip my shawl under you. (*Pause.*) Is that better?

HENRY: No comparison, no comparison. (*Pause.*) Are you going to sit down beside me?

ADA: Yes. (*No sound as she sits.*) Like that? (*Pause.*) Or do you prefer like that? (*Pause.*) You don't care. (*Pause.*) Chilly enough I imagine, I hope you put on your jaegers. (*Pause.*) Did you put on your jaegers, Henry?

HENRY: What happened was this, I put them on and then I took them off again and then I put them on again and then I took them off again and then I put them on again and then I—

ADA: Have you them on now?

HENRY: I don't know. (*Pause.*) Hooves! (*Pause. Louder.*) Hooves! (*Sound of hooves walking on hard road. They die rapily away.*) Again!

Hooves as before. Pause.

ADA: Did you hear them?

HENRY: Not well.

ADA: Galloping?

27

HENRY: No. (*Pause.*) Could a horse mark time?

    Pause.

ADA: I'm not sure that I know what you mean.

HENRY: (*irritably*). Could a horse be trained to stand still and mark time with its four legs?

ADA: Oh. (*Pause.*) The ones I used to fancy all did. (*She laughs. Pause.*) Laugh, Henry, it's not every day I crack a joke. (*Pause.*) Laugh, Henry do that for me.

HENRY: You wish *me* to laugh?

ADA: You laughed so charmingly once, I think that's what first attracted me to you. That and your smile. (*Pause.*) Come on, it will be like old times.
    Pause. He tries to laugh, fails.

HENRY: Perhaps I should begin with the smile. (*Pause for smile.*) Did that attract you? (*Pause.*) Now I'll try again. (*Long horrible laugh.*) Any of the old charm there?

ADA: Oh Henry!

    Pause.

HENRY: Listen to it! (*Pause.*) Lips and claws! (*Pause.*) Get away from it! Where it couldn't get at me! The Pampas! What?

ADA: Calm yourself.

HENRY: And I live on the brink of it! Why? Professional obligations? (*Brief laugh.*) Reasons of health?

(*Brief laugh.*) Family ties? (*Brief laugh.*) A
woman? (*Laugh in which she joins.*) Some old
grave I cannot tear myself away from? (*Pause.*)
Listen to it! What is it like?

ADA: It is like an old sound I used to hear. (*Pause.*) It
is like another time, in the same place. (*Pause.*)
It was rough, the spray came flying over us.
(*Pause.*) Strange it should have been rough then.
(*Pause.*) And calm now.

Pause.

HENRY: Let us get up and go.

ADA: Go? Where? And Addie? She would be very
distressed if she came and found you had gone
without her. (*Pause.*) What do you suppose is
keeping her?

*Smart blow of cylindrical ruler on piano case.
Unsteadily, ascending and descending,* ADDIE
*plays scale of A Flat Major, hands first together,
then reversed. Pause.*

MUSIC MASTER: (*Italian accent*): Santa Cecilia!

Pause.

ADDIE: Will I play my piece now please?

Pause. MUSIC MASTER *beats two bars of waltz
time with ruler on piano case.* ADDIE *plays
opening bars of Chopin's 5th Waltz in A Flat
Major,* MUSIC MASTER *beating time lightly with
ruler as she plays. In first chord of bass, bar 5,
she plays E instead of F. Resounding blow of
ruler on piano case.* ADDIE *stops playing.*

C

MUSIC MASTER: (*violently*). Fa!

ADDIE: (*tearfully*). What?

MUSIC MASTER: (*violently*). Eff! Eff!

ADDIE: (*tearfully*). Where?

MUSIC MASTER: (*violently*). Qua! (*He thumps note.*) Fa!

> *Pause.* ADDIE *begins again,* MUSIC MASTER *beating time lightly with ruler. When she comes to bar 5 she makes same mistake. Tremendous blow of ruler on piano case.* ADDIE *stops playing, begins to wail.*

MUSIC MASTER: (*frenziedly*). Eff! Eff! (*He hammers note.*) Eff! (*He hammers note.*) Eff!

> *Hammered note, "Eff!" and* ADDIE'S *wail amplified to paroxysm, then suddenly cut off. Pause.*

ADA: You are silent today.

HENRY: It was not enough to drag her into the world, now she must play the piano.

ADA: She must learn. She shall learn. That—and riding.

> *Hooves walking.*

RIDING MASTER: Now Miss! Elbows in Miss! Hands down Miss! (*Hooves trotting.*) Now Miss! Back straight Miss! Knees in Miss! (*Hooves cantering.*) Now Miss! Tummy in Miss! Chin up Miss! (*Hooves galloping.*) Now Miss! Eyes front Miss! (ADDIE *begins to wail.*) Now Miss! Now Miss!

30

Galloping hooves, "Now Miss!" and ADDIE'S *wail amplified to paroxysm, then suddenly cut off. Pause.*

ADA: What are you thinking of? (*Pause.*) I was never taught, until it was too late. All my life I regretted it.

HENRY: What was your strong point, I forget.

ADA: Oh . . . geometry I suppose, plane and solid. (*Pause.*) First plane, then solid. (*Shingle as he gets up.*) Why do you get up?

HENRY: I thought I might try and get as far as the water's edge. (*Pause. With a sigh.*) And back. (*Pause.*) Stretch my old bones.

Pause.

ADA: Well, why don't you? (*Pause.*) Don't stand there thinking about it. (*Pause.*) Don't stand there staring. (*Pause. He goes towards sea. Boots on shingle, say ten steps. He halts at water's edge. Pause. Sea a little louder. Distant.*) Don't wet your good boots.

Pause.

HENRY: Don't, don't. . . .

Sea suddenly rough.

ADA: (*twenty years earlier, imploring*). Don't! Don't!

HENRY: (*do.* *urgent*). Darling!

ADA: (*do.* *more feebly*). Don't!

HENRY: (*twenty years earlier, exultantly*). Darling!

> *Rough sea.* ADA *cries out. Cry and sea amplified,*
> *cut off. End of evocation. Pause. Sea calm. He*
> *goes back up deeply shelving beach. Boots*
> *laborious on shingle. He halts. Pause. He moves*
> *on. He halts. Pause. Sea calm and faint.*

ADA: Don't stand there gaping. Sit down. (*Pause.*
Shingle as he sits.) On the shawl. (*Pause.*) Are
you afraid we might touch? (*Pause.*) Henry.

HENRY: Yes.

ADA: You should see a doctor about your talking, it's
worse, what must it be like for Addie? (*Pause.*)
Do you know what she said to me once, when
she was still quite small, she said, Mummy, why
does Daddy keep on talking all the time? She
heard you in the lavatory. I didn't know what
to answer.

HENRY: Daddy! Addie! (*Pause.*) I told you to tell her I
was praying. (*Pause.*) Roaring prayers at God
and his saints.

ADA: It's very bad for the child. (*Pause.*) It's silly to
say it keeps you from hearing it, it doesn't keep
you from hearing it and even if it does you
shouldn't be hearing it, there must be something
wrong with your brain.

> *Pause.*

HENRY: That! I shouldn't be hearing that!

ADA: I don't think you are hearing it. And if you are
what's wrong with it, it's a lovely peaceful

gentle soothing sound, why do you hate it?
(*Pause*.) And if you hate it why don't you keep
away from it? Why are you always coming
down here? (*Pause*.) There's something wrong
with your brain, you ought to see Holloway,
he's alive still, isn't he?

Pause.

HENRY: (*wildly*). Thuds, I want thuds! Like this! (*He
fumbles in the shingle, catches up two big stones
and starts dashing them together*.) Stone! (*Clash.*)
Stone! (*Clash. 'Stone!' and clash amplified, cut
off. Pause. He throws one stone away. Sound of
its fall*.) That's life! (*He throws the other stone
away. Sound of its fall*.) Not this . . . (*pause*) . . .
sucking!

ADA: And why life? (*Pause*.) Why life, Henry?
(*Pause*.) Is there anyone about?

HENRY: Not a living soul.

ADA: I thought as much. (*Pause*.) When we longed
to have it to ourselves there was always
someone. Now that it does not matter the place
is deserted.

HENRY: Yes, you were always very sensitive to being
seen in gallant conversation. The least feather of
smoke on the horizon and you adjusted your
dress and became immersed in the *Manchester
Guardian*. (*Pause*.) The hole is still there, after
all these years. (*Pause. Louder*.) The hole is still
there.

33

ADA: What hole? The earth is full of holes.

HENRY: Where we did it at last for the first time.

ADA: Ah yes, I think I remember. (*Pause.*) The place has not changed.

HENRY: Oh yes it has, *I* can see it. (*Confidentially.*) There is a levelling going on! (*Pause.*) What age is she now?

ADA: I have lost count of time.

HENRY: Twelve? Thirteen? (*Pause.*) Fourteen?

ADA: I really could not tell you, Henry.

HENRY: It took us a long time to have her. (*Pause.*) Years we kept hammering away at it. (*Pause.*) But we did it in the end. (*Pause. Sigh.*) We had her in the end. (*Pause.*) Listen to it! (*Pause.*) It's not so bad when you get out on it. (*Pause.*) Perhaps I should have gone into the merchant navy.

ADA: It's only on the surface, you know. Underneath all is as quiet as the grave. Not a sound. All day, all night, not a sound.

Pause.

HENRY: Now I walk about with the gramophone. But I forgot it today.

ADA: There is no sense in that. (*Pause.*) There is no sense in trying to drown it. (*Pause.*) See Holloway.

Pause.

HENRY: Let us go for a row.

ADA: A row? And Addie? She would be very distressed if she came and found you had gone for a row without her. (*Pause.*) Who were you with just now? (*Pause.*) Before you spoke to me.

HENRY: I was trying to be with my father.

ADA: Oh. (*Pause.*) No difficulty about that.

HENRY: I mean I was trying to get him to be with me. (*Pause.*) You seem a little cruder than usual today, Ada. (*Pause.*) I was asking him if he had ever met you, I couldn't remember.

ADA: Well?

HENRY: He doesn't answer any more.

ADA: I suppose you have worn him out. (*Pause.*) You wore him out living and now you are wearing him out dead. (*Pause.*) The time comes when one cannot speak to you any more. (*Pause.*) The time will come when no one will speak to you at all, not even complete strangers. (*Pause.*) You will be quite alone with your voice, there will be no other voice in the world but yours. (*Pause.*) Do you hear me?

Pause.

HENRY: I can't remember if he met you.

ADA: You know he met me.

HENRY: No, Ada, I don't know, I'm sorry, I have forgotten almost everything connected with you.

ADA: You weren't there. Just your mother and sister.

35

I had called to fetch you, as arranged. We were
to go bathing together.

Pause.

HENRY: (*irritably*). Drive on, drive on! Why do people
always stop in the middle of what they are
saying?

ADA: None of them knew where you were. Your bed
had not been slept in. They were all shouting at
one another. Your sister said she would throw
herself off the cliff. Your father got up and went
out, slamming the door. I left soon afterwards
and passed him on the road. He did not see me.
He was sitting on a rock looking out to sea. I
never forgot his posture. And yet it was a
common one. You used to have it sometimes.
Perhaps just the stillness, as if he had been
turned to stone. I could never make it out.

Pause.

HENRY: Keep on, keep on! (*Imploringly.*) Keep it going,
Ada, every syllable is a second gained.

ADA: That's all, I'm afraid. (*Pause.*) Go on now with
your father or your stories or whatever you
were doing, don't mind me any more.

HENRY: I can't! (*Pause.*) I can't do it any more!

ADA: You were doing it a moment ago, before you
spoke to me.

HENRY: (*angrily*). I can't do it any more now! (*Pause.*)
Christ!

Pause.

ADA: Yes, you know what I mean, there are attitudes
remain in one's mind for reasons that are clear,
the carriage of a head for example, bowed when
one would have thought it should be lifted, and
vice versa, or a hand suspended in mid-air, as if
unowned. That kind of thing. But with your
father sitting on the rock that day nothing of
the kind, no detail you could put your finger on
and say, How very peculiar! No, I could never
make it out. Perhaps, as I said, just the great
stillness of the whole body, as if all the breath
had left it. (*Pause.*) Is this rubbish a help to you,
Henry? (*Pause.*) I can try and go on a little if
you wish. (*Pause.*) No? (*Pause.*) Then I think
I'll be getting back.

HENRY: Not yet! You needn't speak. Just listen. Not
even. Be with me. (*Pause.*) Ada! (*Pause. Louder.*)
Ada! (*Pause.*) Christ! (*Pause.*) Hooves! (*Pause.
Louder.*) Hooves! (*Pause.*) Christ! (*Long pause.*)
Left soon afterwards, passed you on the road,
didn't see her, looking out to. . . . (*Pause.*)
Can't have been looking out to *sea*. (*Pause.*)
Unless you had gone round the other side.
(*Pause.*) Had you gone round the cliff side?
(*Pause.*) Father! (*Pause.*) Must have I suppose.
(*Pause.*) Stands watching you a moment, then on
down path to tram, up on open top and sits
down in front. (*Pause.*) Sits down in front.
(*Pause.*) Suddenly feels uneasy and gets down
again, conductor: 'Changed your mind, Miss?',
goes back up path, no sign of you. (*Pause.*)
Very unhappy and uneasy, hangs round a bit,

not a soul about, cold wind coming in off sea,
goes back down path and takes tram home.
(*Pause.*) Takes tram home. (*Pause.*) Christ!
(*Pause.*) 'My dear Bolton. . . .' (*Pause.*) 'If it's
an injection you want, Bolton, let down your
trousers and I'll give you one, I have a
panhysterectomy at nine,' meaning of course the
anaesthetic. (*Pause.*) Fire out, bitter cold, white
world, great trouble, not a sound. (*Pause.*)
Bolton starts playing with the curtain, no,
hanging, difficult to describe, draws it back, no,
kind of gathers it towards him and the moon
comes flooding in, then lets it fall back, heavy
velvet affair, and pitch black in the room, then
towards him again, white, black, white, black,
Holloway: 'Stop that for the love of God,
Bolton, do you want to finish me?' (*Pause.*)
Black, white, black, white, maddening thing.
(*Pause.*) Then he suddenly strikes a match,
Bolton does, lights a candle, catches it up above
his head, walks over and looks Holloway full in
the eye. (*Pause.*) Not a word, just the look, the
old blue eye, very glassy, lids worn thin, lashes
gone, whole thing swimming, and the candle
shaking over his head. (*Pause.*) Tears? (*Pause.
Long laugh.*) Good God no! (*Pause.*) Not a
word, just the look, the old blue eye, Holloway:
'If you want a shot say so and let me get to hell
out of here.' (*Pause.*) 'We've had this before,
Bolton, don't ask me to go through it again.'
(*Pause.*) Bolton: 'Please!' (*Pause.*) 'Please!'
(*Pause.*) 'Please, Holloway!' (*Pause.*) Candle
shaking and guttering all over the place, lower

now, old arm tired, takes it in the other hand
and holds it high again, that's it, that was always
it, night, and the embers cold, and the glim
shaking in your old fist, saying, Please! Please!
(*Pause.*) Begging. (*Pause.*) Of the poor. (*Pause.*)
Ada! (*Pause.*) Father! (*Pause.*) Christ! (*Pause.*)
Holds it high again, naughty world, fixes
Holloway, eyes drowned, won't ask again, just
the look, Holloway covers his face, not a sound,
white world, bitter cold, ghastly scene, old men,
great trouble, no good. (*Pause.*) No good.
(*Pause.*) Christ! (*Pause. Shingle as he gets up. He
goes towards sea. Boots on shingle. He halts.
Pause. Sea a little louder.*) On. (*Pause. He moves
on. Boots on shingle. He halts at water's edge.
Pause. Sea a little louder.*) Little book. (*Pause.*)
This evening. . . . (*Pause.*) Nothing this evening.
(*Pause.*) Tomorrow . . . tomorrow . . . plumber at
nine, then nothing. (*Pause. Puzzled.*) Plumber at
nine? (*Pause.*) Ah yes, the waste. (*Pause.*) Words.
(*Pause.*) Saturday . . . nothing. Sunday . . .
Sunday . . . nothing all day. (*Pause.*) Nothing,
all day nothing. (*Pause.*) All day all night
nothing. (*Pause.*) Not a sound.

Sea.